MWES Writing Colors Our World 2012-2013

Writing pieces presented by the students of
Mt. Washington Elementary School

Cover artwork by Nolan Hunt, 1st grade

Table of Contents

Nature
By Olivia Armstrong

Nature is free…
Like birds in the sky.

Nature is full of life…
Like a new born child.

Nature is bright…
Like the sun on a cloudless day.

Nature is peaceful…
Like a starry night.

Nature is magnificent…
Like a blooming flower.

Nature is…
God's creation.

The Bully

By: Emily Moats, Abigail Martincic, and Makayla Powers

Bully: Tori Chamber
Bus driver: Mrs. Shana
New girl: McKenna Claire
Girl McKenna meets: Emma rose
Counselor: Mrs. Franklin
Teacher: Mrs.L.Foster
Dad: Troy Claire
Mom: Ashlee
Claire

(McKenna sits in chair)

(Tori comes over)

Tori: (sassy) That is my chair.

McKenna: Sorry I didn't know.

Tori: I know you are new here but MOVE!

Emma: What about you move, Tori.

(The class leaves)

Mrs. L. foster: McKenna are you ok?

McKenna: Yeah I'm ok.

(Last class)

(Getting on bus)

Tori: (sassy) We have assigned seats on the bus so MOVE!

McKenna: Why do I have to move?

Tori: Because the seat doesn't belong to you.

Emma: Tori, it doesn't belong to you either.

Mrs. Shana: Please come up here, McKenna.

McKenna: Am I in trouble?

Mrs. Shana: No, I need to talk to you about assigned seats. Who's your friend?

McKenna: Emma

Mrs. Shana: Go sit by Emma and that's your new assigned seat.

(McKenna smiles)

(They ride for 20 mins)

Mrs. Shana: McKenna, it's your stop

McKenna: Ok!

Tori: (Sassy) Bye McKenna!

McKenna: See you tomorrow!

(Emma and McKenna get off the bus)

(Walks in the house)

Mom Ashlee and Dad Troy: How was your first day at school?

McKenna: It was horrible; There was a girl who was a b-b-bully!

Mom: So how should we handle this, so it stops?

McKenna: I know, let's talk to the counselors.

Emma: I'll go with you to talk to her.

Mom: Yeah, why don't you?

(Next day)

(In the counselor's room)

Mrs. Franklin: So, McKenna and Emma what do you need?

Emma: We need to talk about something that's happening to McKenna.

Mrs. Franklin: So, what's happening McKenna?

McKenna: There is a girl who is being mean to me.

Emma: Well I guess you could she is a bully.

Mrs. Franklin: Well tell me what's happening to you

McKenna: Well when I sit down she always tells me that's her seat, then she tells me I have to move. She also, calls me names.

Mrs. Franklin: Well, who is it that has been calling you all that stuff?

McKenna: t-t-t

Emma: TORI!!!!!!!!!!!!!!!!!!!!!

Mrs. Franklin: oh, I'll have to have a talk with tori.

(leaves office)

Intercom: Tori chamber please report to the counselor's office Tori chamber.

Mrs. Franklin: so, I know that you have had a rough time but that is not a reason you should be a bully to others.

Tori: I understand that.

Mrs. Franklin so will this stop?

Tori: YES! It will

Intercom: Emma and McKenna please come up to the counselor's office

Tori: sorry you felt like I was a bully to you I'll stop

Emma and McKenna: ok just don't let it happen again

(They go home)

Mom: so did it get better?

McKenna and Emma: its fine now everything is great.

THE END!!!!!!!!!!!!!!!

I Am

Carly Morris 5th grade August 30, 2012

I am creative and bright.
I wonder how God was created.
I hear birds chirping in the morning.
I see an angel blowing me a kiss.
I want to be a doctor when I grow up.
I am creative and bright.
I pretend I am a fairy flying through the sky.
I feel like God is holding my hand.
I touch nature as I explore.
I worry my dog Tanner will pass away soon.
I cry when I get in trouble for doing nothing at all.
I am creative and bright.
I understand that everything happens for a
reason.
I say God is real and that he has a plan for me.
I dream all about going to heaven with Jesus.
I try to be myself.
I hope to be a famous singer and actress someday.
I am creative and bright.

Best loving sis in the world!!!!

By. Madison Fultz

Do you have an older sister? I do and she is like a best friend to me. I hope you and your sister are best friends just like me and my sister.

Alex was short for me. She has brown hair. Alex does not were glasses. Like almost all teens she is always on her phone. She is almost outside all the time.

I remember that we played all the time we would go to the park with each other. We play tag and other games together. Alex could climb higher than me. Now really I can climb higher than her.

My sister would always love me even when we are not talking to each other. That is my relationship with Alex. Alex is important to me because she made me feel better when I was down. When I would fall she would be the first one to take me up to mom. That is why Alex made me feel better when I was hurt or when I was down.

The lesson I learned from Alex is that she made me feel good in myself and to never be down. My sister also taught me to be calm and not so noisy when I want to be. Those are some lessons that she taught me.

Alex is like a best friend to me. Alex and I have a very good relationship that is why I pick my sister Alex as a very good relationship with me in my life.

Near Death
By Andrew Abner
Young Authors District Winner 2013

It started as a warm sunny day, but then something horrible happened!

Drew Walker lives with his mom and dad in a medium sized city called Riverview City. Drew is 9 years old and just got out of 3rd grade. Drew has blonde hair and is tall. He has a best friend named Mark. Mark is 9 and just got out of 3rd grade too.

"My life hasn't been very exciting", Drew always says.

Then one day that they thought was just going to be another summer vacation Tuesday was about to be action packed! It was about 11:00 a.m. Mark was waiting for Drew outside

"Come on Drew," Mark said impatiently.

"I'm coming," protested Drew.

They always go to the big flat field. It has some dead bushes and rocks. It actually used to be a big war field. They play lots of games there. They decided to play kick ball today. They played for 1 hour until it was noon. It was nice and sunny out until big cumulonimbus clouds suddenly approached. They ignored the clouds. Thirty minutes later they heard a siren. They turned around and found a funnel cloud reaching toward the ground. They were paralyzed. (5 seconds later...)

"TORNADO!" they both screamed.

They raced toward Drew's house. CRASH! BANG! KABLAMO! It sounded like a freight train. Mark took cover under a tree, and Drew ran for the flashlights that were in the garage. When Drew came back, the tornado had almost sucked Mark up! He was hanging from a tree branch.

"Ahhh! Help me!"

Drew grabbed a rope that was by the garden shed and untangled it.

"Here catch this," Drew screamed.

Drew threw it to Mark and Mark caught it. Drew started to pull and tug. It didn't work. Mark was terrified! Drew's parents saw him through the window and came out to help. They pulled and tugged, their hands were getting rope burned. Soon you could see people coming out their doors to help. Mark felt better because he knew people cared about him. They pulled and tugged with all their might. The whole city was there! Soon after a lot of pulling Mark's feet were on the ground.

"YAY!" everyone screamed.

Everyone went home but Drew, Mark and Drew's parents went for the storm shelter. BANG!! They slammed and locked the heavy metal door. Mark's eyes were as red as an apple because he was crying earlier and he lost his voice from screaming. Drew looked out the tiny window on the door and saw lots of destruction. The duck ponds were ruined, the tennis courts smashed, and the walking trails and pools also ruined. Drew also saw torn down trees and houses. The tornado had crushed Drew's house. The city looked like a wasteland. The tornado was a long way away now but they could still hear the wind howling. Drew didn't care about his house or anything but he was full of joy that they saved Mark, and he meant it!

Hi! Name is Aaron. I am 8 years old. My mom and dad's name is Mindy and Steven. I also have an annoying little brother name David. One of our favorite things to do is play our DS. Actually it is a Nintendo DsI-xl. Mine is red and my brother's is blue

The problem began when my brother had one of the information cards. He of it had too long of a time. I went into his room and took the card out of his and switched the it with Diddy knog versus Marion Mayhem while he was out of his room. The reason I went did this while he was out was because I knew he would throw a big fit. Went to play his dsI-xl when to play his dsI-xl when he in the car... He threw a big fit. I thought myself. "I knew this was going to happen." My mommy said "David way are you acting like you are 3 year old?" David said "while he was crying and mad, "Aaron switched the card and took it!" Mom replied Aaron did you do that?" Aaron said yes because he has had it for too long!" Mom said that's right I forgot to tell Aaron it was his turn."

If you and your brother could learn to work out your problems you wouldn't lose time on your dsI-xl David and I decided we would try to work on sharing and not awing all time

Rocket

By: Eleanor Bandy

Hello my name is Ella. I am 8 years old. I love Science stuff.

I live at my aunt's house. She is a scientist. She has a rocket in her lab. I have always *not* "wanted" to ride a rocket. Ok I think it's great!

"Hey mom, can I go get some chips?"

"Yes, you can," mom said.

Well that fooled her. Ok let's find that rocket. Where is it? Wow! I found it! It's so big. How do you get in this thing? Oh here it is. Inside is so big. Wow! What are these buttons...what is this one? I am in a seat.

My mom came looking for me and she finally saw me in the rocket. "Wait!" mom said, "Wait! Where are you going?"

"I'm going to the moon," I said.

"How are you going to get home?" mom said. I roared away in the rocket before she could stop me. It seemed like a couple of days and finally I saw the moon. I am glad the rocket was on auto pilot.

I put on a space suit and climbed down the ladder of the rocket.

"I'm at the moon," I thought to myself. "This is so cool but what is that rumbling? What!? Where did the rocket go? She looked over and the rocket was gone. Oh no. I lost the rocket!"

How am I going to get home? I thought about it for a minute.

That's it! I will just jump down off the moon…. I think. Ok let's go! I took a running start and HERE I GO… WWWWOOOOOO! Good thing I had a parachute and space boots. I think I broke my spine. I'm good now. Let's get home.

"Mmmmooooommm," Ella said.

"Sweetie," mom exclaimed hugging me. "There you are. I missed you so much. You're aunt just got home from the market."

Ding Dong! "I'm home," said her aunt. "You will never believe what I heard. There has been a terrible accident. Someone said a rocket fell on a house in our neighborhood."

"You're kidding," I thought. "How was I going to explain this? I might need to find another rocket and go back to the moon because I am probably going to be grounded for life!

The end

THE MONSTER TRUCK SHOW

By Alec Brady

One day me and my family and my friends went to a truck show. Our friends weren't there yet so we went in and we bought the wrong tickets. So we went to get some but they were out of tickets. So we waited for our friends to see if they had extra.

While we were waiting we went to a boat show. And we looked around and finally they came and gave us some tickets.

We got the tickets and we went in. During the show there were these two transformers that were fighting. Both of them were from two different planets.

So they kept on fighting and the good guy won. And then the monster trucks came out to race. Grave digger won the whole thing. After that the grave digger driver came in our stands and gave someone a remote control monster truck to someone.

After the race, the drivers introduced themselves. My favorite driver was grave digger.

After that I wanted a signing but it was a long line. So we left. That was the time I went to a monster truck show.

3 Little Fish

By Ryan Daugherty

Once upon a time, 3 little fish loved to be with each other. But one day they met a big bad shark that loved to eat fish. So they are going to houses.

So, the first fish built a house out of seaweed. The shark came over, knock, knock, knock, "yes let me come in not by the hair on my finny fin fin. I'm going to eat you ahh!" the other fish made his house out of bones of dead fish. The shark came over and said, let me come in. not by the hair on my finny fin fin. "I'm going to blow your house down, no"

So, the smartest fish built his house out of an old dock that has fallen in the water. The two other fish swam too the house and said, "Brother please help us, the big bad shark is coming,"

"Hide!" said the fish!

The fish swam quickly under the bed. The shark came to the door. **Knock knock knock,** "let me come in." "Not by the hair on my finny fin

fin." I'm coming in. the fish heard a bang on the door.

The shark tried to get in the house but it was too hard. He swam up the house were the chimney was, the fish saw him and got a baseball bat.

The shark went to the chimney, he went down the chimney and the fish wacked in the mouth and made his teeth fall out. Every fish was chering.

The end

HEALTHY HORSE
By Karley Davis

Howdy, my name is Elizabeth but I like to be called Liz. I am 18 years old and I live in a barn. I have braided brown hair, I'm 6 foot 5 inches and I wear cow girl boots. I like horseback riding. I really care about my mom, dad and my horse named Chance. I like to spend most of my time in the barn and the fied. I've never told anybody about my horse. She is having a baby.

One day Elizabeth was coming home from school and she stopped by her barn to check on Chance, her horse. But when she saw her horse was getting bigger in the stomach, Elizabeth knew that she had to tell her mom and dad that Chance was having a baby.

The next day, Elizabeth went to tell her mom and dad that Chance was having a baby and Elizabeth was nervous. Elizabeth said to herself, "Here I go into the kitchen to tell my mom and dad." So she goes into the kitchen and said to her mom and dad, "Chance is having a baby!" said Elizabeth.

"That's funny sweet heart but what's the real thing you want to tell us," said mom.

"That was the real thing," said Elizabeth.

"Then we need to get prepared," said Elizabeth's dad.

"Okay," said mom.

The next day they went to the store and bought things for the baby horse. "Can I name the baby horse?" Elizabeth asked.

"Yes you can," said Elizabeth's dad.

The next day Elizabeth asked her dad, "Is the horse a healthy horse?"

"I'm sure it is," said Elizabeth's dad.

The last day of school, Elizabeth came home and the baby horse was born. Elizabeth was so exiled she went and told mom and dad. "Dad did you see the foal?" said Elizabeth.

They took the baby horse to Elizabeth's uncle's house. Elizabeth's uncle said, "She is a healthy foal."

Everyone hollered together, "Hooray," and went back to Elizabeth's house and everyone was happy.

THE END

Katie's Sculpture

By Chloe Duke

Crack "Oh no"! Katie screamed as her brother Sam had gotten something very important.

One day there was a girl named Katie Greenwell. She is 12 years old. Katie lives in a small house by a big creek that has a lot of fish. Katie has freckles and curly brown hair. She has a horse named Zoey, a tea cup pig named Piglet, and a dog named Rose Bud. She does not talkback. She takes care of older adults. Katie likes to do crafts for people.

Katie screamed that day because her brother Sam had broken her clay sculpture from when she was in first grade. It had 5 yellow stars on it. Katie went into her Hello Kitty room and sat on her Hello Kitty bed. She was trying to solve this. First she tried to glue it, but the parts fell off. Then she tried to tape it, but the parts were hanging off like a broken spider web.

"Are you alright"? Asked mom.

"My clay sculpture, Sam broke it!" said Katie as tears dropped down her face.

Then she went to ask her dad if she could make pottery with him.

"Yeah I would love to make pottery with you," said Katie's dad.

"Ok well I will go in the kitchen and wait for you," said Katie as she walked in the kitchen. Then dad walked in. He had a bunch of clay.

"Wow!" said Katie proudly. And Katie and her dad made a cup for her brother but he broke this cup. Katie made more until he learned not to break things.

Pigs

By Isaac Gray

Hello my name is Sky, I live in minecraft in a brick hose with some pigs and I like experimenting with the pigs. Sometimes I go to the top of my house and watch the sunrise. The rise looks very cool, all those monsters on fire, items on the ground. That's pretty much what happens.

This particular day in minecraft I was thinking about   pigs and pig related things. So I flew up to the top of my house and spawned 500 guinea pigs and tamed them with apples. When I went into my house it was crowded with guinea pigs and pigs so we went on a trip.

GIVE IT BACK!

By Mickenna Harthun

One day a little girl named Maddy lived on a horse ranch with her sister Tori and her Mom and Dad. Oh! Her dog Lily too. Maddy fell off her horse a few weeks ago and was hurt very badly. Maddy can't wait to get back on the horse but now her mom won't let her ride her horse.

Maddy's mom had decided to give the horse to Tori, Maddy's older sister. She felt that Tori was older and more responsible.

Maddy was very unhappy about this decision. She knew that she would be alright to ride her horse again. If her mom didn't let her back on the horse, she thought she might die. She loved horses.

"Mom, please can I get back on my horse?" said Maddy.

"No, I don't want you getting hurt!" said her mom.

"But mom I won't! Please don't give my horse to Tori...it isn't right!" Maddy cried.

"Go to your room!" her mom said.

"But mom," stammered Maddy.

"Go!" said her mom.

So she went to her room so mad that she was crying! She flopped down on her bed and thought about what she should do. When Maddy finally calmed down, her phone rang. It was Kayla and she said, "Do you what to go horseback riding?"

Maddy said, "I wish I could but my mom won't let me." "Oh right, I have an idea" said Kayla. She whispered the plan to Maddy.

So Kayla came over to get Tori, Maddy's sister, to tell her the plan. She wanted Tori to tell her mom to give Maddy back her horse back. Tori didn't really want the horse because she was too much of a girly girl. Kayla, Tori and Maddy all went down stars to the living room. "Mom, I think Maddy should get her horse back. I don't even want the horse." said Tori.

Mrs. Harthun thought about her quick decision to not let Maddy ride her horse ever again. She knew that if Maddy didn't get back on her horse, she might be too scared to ever ride her horse again. She was just afraid to let anything bad happen to her girls. So she finally answered her daughter....

"Yes! I was just so worried about you when you got hurt. I don't know what I would do without you!"

"Yay!" Maddy screamed!

"I'm happy for you" said Kayla. "Now do you want to ride horses?" Everyone laughed. Maddy and her family were happy. They celebrated by riding their horses.

The end

Not Here, Not There

By: Emma Hays

Sob Sob

"I can't believe I lost it. Wait, what was that noise?" mentioned Penny.

Penny has brown hair and eyes. She liked to be outside and to listen to music. She lives in Mt. Washington with her brother Lane and mom Nicole. Penny loved her family and all animals.

Penny was Lane's favorite sibling until that Sunday. Penny was outside. It was so hot it felt like she was in an oven so her mom was cleaning Mr. Cool's cage and Penny was so bored because she had nothing to do so she gets Mr. Cool out of the cage. They play all day long until they play hide-n-seek. She could not find Mr. Cool. She looked everywhere inside and outside, behind trees, and upstairs but she could not find him.

Penny made a fake one out of clay and maybe he won't notice that Mr. Cool is gone but it looked nothing like him. She thought to herself, "I just lost my brothers guinea pig." She really did too so she was going to say the dog or the cat ate it but they are in cages. Penny started to cry. She was so very sad.   She thought, "I'm a very bad girl."

Penny said I'm going to get in so much trouble. Penny's brother Lane came out to play with her and he saw Mr. Cool was gone. Lane got mad at Penny.

Penny told Lane "I'm so sorry."

Penny and Lane went down to the pet store to go get another guinea pig.

Lane told Penny, "Name him Mr. Cool."

Penny laughed.

Tears, Go Away

By: Braedyn Hiemer

One ordinary day, Rebecka was walking through the school lunch room. "OH NO!"

Rebecka Raine Leslie is 8 years old and has long brown hair. She was really small so she got bullied a lot. She didn't fight back because she was too small. She was walking fast through the school lunch room at the end of the day. The walls were as blue as the sky. She was just hoping to not get bullied.

Rebecka was passing the Writers Wall of Fame when the biggest bully in school walked up. His name is Jim. He stood beside her.

"No! Stop! Please stop! ," Rebecka screamed.

"Ha! Ha! You really think I'm going to stop," Jim said in a mean voice. Then, BAM! Jim punched her in the stomach right there inside of school.

"OOWW", Rebecka cried. When she went home she didn't know what to do the next day.

"What's wrong sweetie?" her parents asked concerned.

"Oh nothing!" Rebecka groaned.

When she got into the school building the next day she ran to the counselor's office. The walls were sunshine yellow.

"Ms. Lexer, why was Jim in here?" she asked.

"Well." Ms. Lexer began, "He's having some trouble at home and can't control his temper and he's been bullying people."

"Well... he bullied me and that's why I'm here," Rebecka confessed.

Ms. Lexer and Rebecka had a long conversation about standing up for yourself. Ms. Lexer told some jokes to make her feel better. They also played a game called Shoots and Ladders. After that, Rebecka wasn't afraid to stand up for herself anymore. At the next PowWow Rebecka did a PowerPoint about bullying and standing up for yourself and nobody was bullied at Mt. Washington Elementary School again.

THE BOSS

By Alexis Huff

There once was a girl named Emily. She lived in a big white house with her sister Jade, her mom and her dad. She had blond hair and blue eyes. She had a great smile and was quite nice.

If she had a bad quality it was that she loved to text and show off her phone. She spent a lot of time at recess on her phone and rarely played with anyone. Her phone was her friend.

One day at school on the playground, she was texting without looking at what she was doing. She slipped in a big...MUD PUDDLE! She yelled, "Someone help me up right now!" Some girls in her class ran over laughing.

"Quit laughing at me," Emily cried. The girls finally stopped laughing and everybody gathered around and looked at her. She had a big muddy spot on her pants and her phone was all dirty and wet too. One of the girls reached down and helped her get out of the mud. Emily whined, "I'm a mess and my phone is ruined."

"That's what you get when your best friend is a phone," said the helpful girl.

Emily said, "You know your right." Do you want to be friends with me? "The girl and her friends said, "Sure, if you promise not to text and play with us instead."

It was a hard choice but Emily finally said, "Ok fine I promise I won't text."

The girls and Emily played games all recess long. Emily was never bossy, sassy or texty. Emily thought it felt good to have friends. Emily thought playing games was way better than texting.

Emily became friends with everybody in her class. She never fell again and only texted when she was alone and sitting. She had a lot more friends. Everybody loved the new Emily.

Celebration of the Purple Stains

By: Logan Leake

Boom, Boom, Splash.

Don't drink coke at school; it's for your own good. Trust me. There was a boy named Evan who is 6 years old. He is very mature for his age. Evan has bluish eyes, freckles, and a pimple on his face. It's so big he gets bullied because of it.

Now it started one beautiful day. Evan was getting to school in style like Michael Jackson. As soon as he walked in he wasn't Michael Jackson any more. Evan heard laughing from Joey, the school bully. Evan was heartbroken when Joey said, "Little twerp, you never pulled a prank. I triple dog dare you to shake up your dad's coke."

Evan had steam coming out of his ears. Evan was mad because Drew, Evan's friend told everybody Evan's secret that he never pulled a prank.

When Evan got home he tried to shake up his dad's Coke to calm Evan down. Then Evan came up with an idea. His idea was to give a coke to a kid at school who was making fun of Evan.

Evan wanted to give the Coke to Drew because he told everybody his secret.

It was the day he gave it to Drew and Drew opened it.   Splash, splash! Purple soda exploded on Drew. It stained his shirt purple.

Everyone yelled, "Good one Evan."

Ever since that day, Evan never got made fun of again.

Drew said you had to shake it up on your dad but Evan said "a prank is a prank."

Evan never got made fun of again. Then Evan felt like Mr. Famous when they chanted his name and Evan threw a party of the celebration. There were banners and decorations. Evan never got made fun of again.

Mission Flying Cat
By: Trey Lemon

Chapter 1: Meet Muffins

My name is Muffins. I'm 4 years old. I like to be called the PEANUT BUTTER THUNDER and Bill. I live with my owner and the two children named Billy and Jane. They are 9 and 12 years old. Jane is 9 and Billy is 12. I like to play with yarn and watch planes. My favorite place is by the fire. And right now I'm watching a plane. It makes me want to fly. My owner doesn't like planes, and the noise they make. We live in a mansion with a gold room and 100 other rooms.

Chapter 2: The man of my dreams

One day I was walking in the yard, when I came across a man named Walter. He asked me if I wanted to fly. I said, "Yes." But then my owner came out and said, "No". But Walter talked her into it. And then Walter told me that FCA stands for Flying

Cat Association. And that's where I'm
going.

Chapter 3: The House of the FCA

When I got into the FCA
Headquarters they started singing an
annoying song. I told them to stop and they
kept quiet. I went to the training room.
Almost everything said danger, keep away,
highly toxic. I asked Walter if they were
typos.

Luckily he said, "Yes, we use them to
keep away criminals".

"What kind of criminals?" I asked

"People in the FDA," Walter
exclaimed. "It stands for Flying Dog
Association," said Walter.

I said in my mind, "I wish there weren't any
dogs in this." Walter told me to take a pill
that came with some water. He told me the
pill was tuna flavor. I took it and I was in
mid-air.

Chapter 4: Muffins way to the FDA

"I can fly!" I said to Walter.

"Now you have to beat the FDA," said Walter.

"WHAT!" I said. "I HAVE TO BEAT THE FDA?"

"Yep," said Walter. "Just take this pill and you'll have super strength, laser eyes, and super speed.

"Gimme that pill!" I said.

"But take caution," said Walter. "If you get addicted with so much power you could take over the world."

"Ok," I said and zoomed of with the pill.

Chapter 5: Triumph!

I was looking for the FDA. I spotted them in Central Park in New York. I zoomed in through the window. There where black labs, golden retrievers and Yorkshire terriers. They were all lifting weights. The Yorkshire terriers were on my side. I knew I'd win, when that happened. The black labs were making swift turns through obstacles. They started shouting, "Intruder, intruder!" I flew through the obstacles. Then I saw the master, Dr. Rogers. He was making collars, the ones I saw on the dogs. But the terriers weren't hypnotized. He turned his chair and I hid behind a silver machine. The terriers distracted him while I headed toward the power source.

I used my laser eyes to break it, and it worked. I broke it! Dr. Rogers saw me, but not in time, he called the dogs. Luckily I could teleport. The collars stopped coming, the dogs stopped, and boss stopped. Like a flood, everybody shouted "FCA, FCA!" I went back to the FCA and everybody crowded me. They shouted "Muffins, Muffins." I asked if they had room for 5 more cat fans. Billy and Jane came and hugged me as hard as they could. After that Walter said, "Yes". And once again the FCA rose above all.

☺ THE END ☺

There's Santa

By Kaelyn Lentz

My name is Kaelyn Lentz. I live in a little, old house. I have blue eyes and blonde hair. I am 8 years old. I have 1 brother and 2 parents and a lot of people in my family. "You probably don't know this but I wondered what I was going to get for Christmas?"

My family, grandparents, aunts, uncles, and cousins all went to sit down and pray before we eat. "What do you want to eat?" said mom.

"I want some turkey some ham and some corn with mash potatoes and some sweet potatoes," I said.

"Wow you will not be hungry later," mom said.

"I know," I said.

The next day, Santa is stuck on top of my house and I see one of his reindeer because I went out and played in the snow. "Hi little girl. What is your name?" said Santa.

"Kaelyn Lentz. Are you Santa and are you stuck on my house?"

"Why yes, I am stuck on top of your house and I am Santa." "Wow mom is that really Santa?" I asked.

"Well sure it is," she said.

"I can't believe it is really Santa," I said happily.

"Mom is that really Santa or are you joking?" I said.

"No I am not joking!" said mom.

"WOW!" I said. "Santa, would you like to have hot chocolate with us?" I say.

"Yes, yes, yes I would but first how am I going to have to get down," said Santa.

"I know what just to do," I say.

"Daddy would you please get out the ladder for Santa?" I say.

"Why sure honey," dad says.

Daddy put the ladder up to the side of the roof for Santa and he climbed down.

"Thank you," I say.

"Thank you," Santa says.

"You're welcome," daddy says. Everyone follows my dad into the house. Daddy leads Santa over to a chair and he sits down. Daddy turns towards the tree and our presents.

"Well let's see what you got," says dad. I carefully open a present. It is a kindle fire.

"You got a kindle fire," says daddy.

"Yay I really wanted that. Thank you very much Santa" I say. I guess I have been a good girl," I say.

"You sure have," said Santa.

"How are you going to get home Santa? Will you be ok?" I say.

"Stop asking all these questions. He's just a man," mom said.   "I'm sorry she is always like this," said mom.
"That's ok," said Santa.

"Every year I get stuck on top of somebody's house. I want to see who is thoughtful enough to help me and invite me into their home." said Santa.

"Your lucky that it was yours," said Santa

"I know. I'm really glad I got to help you this year," I said.   "That is why you received the gift you really wanted," Santa said.

"I hope I will get to see you next year and all I want is to see you! You don't have to bring me anything." I say.

The end!!!

Beep Bop Aliens
By Ashlee Lewis

Up in the sky, on a cold night, lands something strange. Beep bop.

Once there was a boy named Ethan Leo Carpenter. Ethan is 8 years old and lives with his mom and dad on Anoka Street in Tasmania, Australia. Ethan has black hair, tall & wears a St. Louis Cardinals baseball cap. Ethan once went to space camp, his leader was Space Ranger 69 but he had to leave 2 years ago before camp was over. Ethan thought he would never see Space Ranger 69 until one day Ethan saw a light in the sky.

Ethan creeps out to see what it was. By his surprise it was a UFO! Ethan was lucky that the aliens didn't see him. Ethan creeps back to tell mom and dada but they don't believe him.

"Go back to bed Ethan," mom said in a very sleepy voice.

Now Ethan pretends he goes back to sleep but he actually goes back to take a picture. But again mom and dad don't believe him because he has a collection of UFO pictures. Also, this does look like one of his pictures. This one looks like a rectangle with 5 blinking yellow lights. But then it just got harder because more landed and aliens started to come out. The aliens were pink and green, tall and 3 black eyes. Just then, Ethan remembered that aliens go after light and you can destroy them by destroying their solar panel in there UFO. So Ethan creeps back to get a glow stick and his bat. Ethan throws the glow stick out the window and runs to destroy the solar panels. Matter of fact, Ethan destroyed them just in time before the aliens captured him. Then one more UFO landed and it was Space Ranger 69!

"Thank you son for saving the town from the aliens," thanked Space Ranger.

"No problem Space Ranger even though it was kind of hard because mom and dad didn't help", explained Ethan.

"Ethan, do you want to come to the space station with me?" asked Space Ranger.

"Yes, I do Space Ranger! Let's go ask mom and dad," Ethan said in a joyful voice.

"Hi Space Ranger 69! Glad to see you again. What have you been up to?" asked mom.

"Lezzy, can Ethan come to the Space Station with me?" asked Space Ranger 69.

"Ethan can go to the Station if we can go to," exclaimed mom!

"Ok mom," Ethan said in an excited voice.

They all lived happily ever after in the space station for 2 or 3 years and Ethan grows up to be like Space Ranger 69 and everyone is happy.

Trick or Treating

By Samuel Mann

Hi my   is Sam I live at my house with my
dog and my guinea pig Charlie. Before we went
trick-or-treating I had to pick out a costume for
Halloween but it only took 15 minutes I finely I
picked a man bat costume so we had time to
get candy we picked tootsie rolls and tear
jerkers gum.

We got there just in time. we went around twice
and got a lot of candy but mostly from my mom
so we had a sour gum chewing compaction. It
was fun but after I cried.

So after we went trick-or-treating we went home
to drink soda and play GAME BANG!

But little did know my dog Finn was in the game
room with our candy. he was dashing faster then
a chicken hulk.

He came dashing out but my sister was watching
TV but then we remembered the double doors
so we each went on one side but my cousin cout
him.

So that's my story.

Magic dog

By Rachael May

Once there was a boy named Jack, who was 6 years old. His dad had a magic dog name Coco. Well the only way to get the dog was to whistle. But Jack didn't know how to whistle.

There is another boy named Danny. Well the big guy, Danny, does <u>NOT</u> own the magic dog but he <u>CAN</u> whistle. Danny's whistle sounded like, "WWWWHHHIISSSSTTLE!" All that Jacks could get out was, "hhhhhhiiiiiss." So Jack ran home and begged, "Daddy please teach me!?" "Teach you what?" said his dad. "How to whistle," exclaimed Jack.

That night the window opened in Jack's room, "ruff ruff" barked Coco. "Coco!" said Jack. "Why did you come? I can't whistle," said Jack. "That's ok," said Coco. "Coco you talked!" said Jack surprisingly. "Jack who are you talking to up there!" said his dad mad that he was not asleep. "No one I'm talking to myself!" said Jack. Then Jack heard a *Whoosh*. Coco was gone "<u>NO</u>!" said Jack crying.

Jack couldn't sleep, "I want just one wish," said Jack. *Whoosh.* Coco came in to Jack's room.

"I forgot to give you a wish," said Coco.

"I wish my dad would teach me how to whistle," said Jack.

So next thing you know..."Jack," said his dad. "Come down here." Just then dad said, "You put your hands up like this and blow!"

The next day, he whistled and the dog and boy lived happily ever after.

The end

The Hunt

By Jordan McCubbins

Squeak! Squeak!

"Baylee what is that noise?" Jordan questioned.

Baylee Danielle Meeks always has a pink or purple barrette in her thick brown hair. Baylee Danielle Meeks is a six-teen year old girl in high school and dresses nice. Baylee loves to shop with her mom and her little sister named Jordan. Baylee has sparkling green eyes like grass. Baylee feeds her hamsters named Chocolate Chip and Oreo. Oreo and Chocolate Chip are all white with black spots and have black beady eyes.

"They escaped!" Baylee screamed.

We knew the hamsters were missing because their cage was empty and we heard a squeak noise and it wasn't from their cage.

Baylee and her younger sister Jordan looked and looked. They couldn't find them. Baylee and Jordan both were very sad and worried.

"Baylee, you go look upstairs and I'll go look downstairs," concluded Jordan.

"Come here little fella. Where are you?" asked Baylee.

Baylee found them upstairs in their dad's room under a dresser.

They were worried because there dog was running and could've eaten them. Ruff Ruff Ruff!

When they found them upstairs they couldn't get to them because the dresser was to low so Jordan told Baylee to dress up in her favorite hamster costume that was black and white with black beady eyes like the hamsters and act like she was eating hamster food. Then the hamsters came out to eat the food. Then Baylee and her younger sister Jordan put the hamsters back in the cage and closed the door so they wouldn't escape ever again.

CHEESE

By Jenna Meeks

There was a girl name Katie. She 7 years old and she lives in a brick house. She likes to play a whole lot of sports. She has friend name Bobby and Paul. Bobby is 8 years old and Paul is 6 years old. Paul, Bobby and Katie all get along really good.

Well one day, the girl named Katie, was at school. She was thinking about picture day. She always wanted to stick out her tongue on picture day. This was just an evil thought she had.

"Ok now." said the teacher. Katie was nervous. She was nervous because her mom always dressed her up. She didn't like to wear dress up clothes. She wanted to wear clothes to run and play and get dirty in.

The teacher told everyone to line up. We walked to the gym and got in line. Everyone was smiling and getting their picture taken. Then the whole class would walk over and get a class picture made. The idea of sticking out her tongue was still in her head. She couldn't get rid of the thought. So it came to her class getting their picture taken and she was dressed up and the camera man said, "CHEESE!"

Then her mom said, "Where's the picture from picture day?" "Um." said Katie. Her friend's took their pictures to their moms. Katie threw her picture in the dog house. She didn't want her mom to see the picture because her face didn't look so good.

A little while later, the dog walks in. Katie sees the picture in his mouth. She snatches the picture put of his mouth before her mom can see it.

She took her picture to her room. She carefully pulled out a red marker. She drew red tongues on everyone. She did this to make it look like everybody was sticking out there tongue. Her mom would never know she was sticking out her tongue.

THE END

The Election

By Gracie Merkle

Hi! my name is Gracie I live with my mom, brothers, sister and dad. I live in a house that is red, orange, black and yellow. I have a pink and black shirt and I have yellow hair and wear glasses and I live in a white house.

The elation for president was about to start me and this guy Lincoln was in the elation I said "what are you doing here" he said I am running for president". What are you doing here" said Lincoln. I am running for president too "said Gracie.

"Well you better let me win" said Gracie. Maybe I will let you win or maybe I will not let you win. Well said Lincoln are you nice? Said Lincoln. Yes said Gracie.

Ok I let 1,000 people vote for you. Lincoln said for the elation I will make more busies schools and laws. For the elation Gracie said I will make more parks and football fields.

Lincoln you can go home Gracie go get your family you are living in the white house.

Ghosty and Kendall
By Kendell Parish

Chapter 1

My name is Ghosty. I am a ghost dog. You can tell why my name is Ghosty. I live in a grave next to my puppy Muffins. My friend Kendall and her wolf Silver are helping me get into heaven. We need to get a gem from a haunted mansion that has a BUNCH of ghosts. Just because I'm a ghost doesn't mean I'm not scared of them. If we show the gem to the god he will open the gate to heaven!

Chapter 2

The first thing that happened was I was just minding my own business when I heard a shovel. I was quiet. Muffins was whimpering. Just then I heard a BOOM!!!!!!!! Then Kendall and Silver(Kendall's Wolf) came out. I yelled at her, "WHAT?! IT WAS

YOU!?" "Whoa whoa! I didn't mean anything! Did we Silver?" "Huh uh." "Oh. Sorry I went all cranky on you. So, what do you want?" I asked. Kendall replied, "We just wanted to see how things were going." I said back, "EVERYTHINGS GOING BAD!" I sobbed, "I'm so lonely! Well, I guess not THAT lonely with Muffins. I want to be with more of my own kind. Can you help me get into heaven?" Kendall replied, "Sure, we'll help you. Won't we Silver?"

Chapter 3

We had to go to a few places before we reached the mansion. "Uhhhhg. This is taking forever!! I have homework to do! I'm totally going to get a F on it!" complained Kendall. "Stop complaining Kendall. We'll only be a few hours."

3 Hours later...

"Here we are!" I said "The swamp!" "The what?" asked Kendall. "The swamp. We're supposed to find a key in the green stuff." I said "WHAT!? IN THE GOO!? NO WAY MAN!!!!!!" Kendall screamed in disgust. "I will go. All people who went in the never came out. I'm a ghost."

15 minutes later...

"Got it! Also found this bone! Yummy." I munched on the bone. I didn't notice it was a skeleton bone until Kendall screamed, "DUDE!!!!!!! THAT'S A SKELETON BONE!!!!!!" I was disgusted when I looked at it.

Chapter 4

We were at the gate of the haunted mansion. All we needed was a key! But unfortunately, there was no key in sight. "Well... I could just fly over the gate and

unlock it!" I suggested. "Yeah that's a good idea!" Kendall said. "RRRRRRRRRRAAAAAAAAAAAAAAAA AAAAAARRRRRRRRRRRRRRRRRRRR RRRRRRRRRRR!!!" "WHAT WAS THAT?!"I yelled. Then I saw distant shadow.
"Kkkkkkkendall?! LOOK BEHIND YOU!!!!!!" I screamed. "Ghosty, trust me there is nothing beh-." Then, when Kendall turns around, there was a GIANT troll standing in front of us.
"AAAAAAAAAAAAAAAAAAAAAAAAHH HHHHHHHHHHHHHH!!!!!!!!" Me and Kendall screamed. "DON'T HURT US! WE JUST WANT TO GET INTO HEAVEN!" Kendall sobbed. I looked down, just then I saw a sudden sparkle on the ground. Then I saw a key!!
"YIPPPEEEEEE!!!! Look Kendall I found a key!" I screamed like it was Christmas and I got a TV. "Wahoooo!" Kendall was so proud of me. "Now I cannot be bored. I can be with more ghost dogs! We

can play tag and..." I looked up at Kendall. She had a tear in her eye. "Don't worry Kendall. We can still text!" I said with a sudden twinkle in my eye. "So all we have to do is get in there and get that diamond!"

Chapter 5

I unlocked the door. There was a creepy creak when I opened the door. I was TERRIFIED of ghosts. If I see 1 ghost, I would hide in the nearest open place. Like a vase. "Okay. In we go. Heh heh!" I gulped. "Dude, don't be scared! It'll be a piece of cake!" Kendall tried to force me into the door. "No! Stop it! I hate ghosts!" I whined. "Dude, don't be a wus." Kendall said. When I heard that first word, I toughened up like if someone was lifting weights for like a week. "Okay I'm going in." I said. When I opened the door to the mansion and my fears melted away. I used my heat sense to

know which room the gem was in.
Just then, I saw a ghostly shadow
lurking down the hall. My spine
tingled. My teeth chattered. But I
just remembered. I toughened up.
I'm not scared of a stupid old
ghost. I am one! So, I flew past the
ghost, down the hall, and into a
sparkling door. I had a happy
face. I could finally play some
ghost dog games! "Finally. I can
go to heaven!" I said to myself. I
picked up the diamond and I
rushed back outside to Kendall.
"GET TO THE GRAVEYARD!
PRONTO!" I got to my grave. I
yelled, "BOOO!!" The god showed
up. "Thanks for my diamond"
Now I am out of paper so this is
officially

THE END

Savanna and cupcake

By Lorelei Redden

Hi my name is savanna and I have curly hair. I like my dog cupcake and my dog has curly hair to. We have a big house with a upstairs and a down stairs.

One day I was playing with my dog and then my mom yelled because company was here. When I came out my dog was gone. I yelled out CUPCAKE CUPCAKE but she didn't come back.

I ran into the house and I told my mom and my dad all about it because I was wired really bad. My mom had an idea she said, "We can make posters". I said" yes" very excited because I think somebody can find my dog.

Next we went to door to door but nobody had my dog so we went to our house and we set on the couch and I went to the phone so maybe someone would my find my dog and then the phone rang I

answered it but nobody found my dog it was the
electric company.

Then the doorbell rang two of my girlfriends came to
my house and said "I find your dog savanna" I said "
You guys are the best" but my mom said' think you"
she said. I thanked my friends again and again.

My mom closeted the door. Then my mom said " Go
and play in your room because she did not want me
to play with cupcake for 1 hour so I went to my
room for 1 hour so I played with my toys and my
mom came in the room and she said" I lost cupcake"'
she said then it started all over

A DAY IN CHINA
By Zachary Sloan

"Hi my name is Kevin. Do you want to hear about the time I made a wrestler mad? It was really easy to make him happy again. Yes, I know him better than anyone. I am the wrestler's coach and his friend. "

Inside a C-130, a soldier was about to jump before the

C-130 hit the cliff ... **BANG**! He jumped. The other soldier, Kevin, fell right behind him. Kevin said, "We are lost! We were blown off course. Let's find a village." They started down the road.

When they finally made it to the village, they decided they were in China. There was a Chinese wrestler at a restaurant. Kevin and the other soldier ran to sit down at the table next to the wrestler. The wrestler said, "Give me that seat or I will hit you!" The two soldiers ran away.   Then they ran into the wrestlers coach.

The coach said." If you are running to get the seat instead of the wrestler, you should have just asked the wrestler if you could in the seat." You should treat others the way you want to be treated.

Bryan's Big Fight

By Jared St. Clair

Crack, bang, boom

Bryan broke his bat he hit a home run no one could believe it

Bryan lives in a house a pretty ordinary house on Flicker Lane. He lives with his mom and dad. He has brown eyes and brown hair. He is always in a baseball shirt and pants. He is 10 years old.

Now here's how it all started. Bryan and his friends were at the baseball park. When it was his turn to bat everybody kept on YELLING at him because he kept striking out. That made him really mad.

Bryan's dad went in there to watch but none of them would listen to him. They just kept yelling. Finally he hit it. Bryan felt good that he actually hit it. His teammates were even cheering him on. It wasn't his turn to bat any more. But the next time it was his turn to bat, the same thing started. "I don't know what to do," Bryan thought.

This time Bryan had an idea because they were still yelling so he went outside of the baseball park and went to each of their parents and told them what they were saying about him. Like "you're not supposed to miss it you're supposed to hit it." They were also saying, "you're never going to hit it."

But after the baseball game, each of them got along just fine.

Jonny The TROLL
By Adam Stewart

One day there was a little troll named Jonny.
He had no friends because nobody liked him.
Nobody liked him because he was ugly. His
face was big and he had big ears. He could
not stop drooling out of the corner of his
mouth. So you can see why he had no
friends. Except one boy and his name was
Ben.

Ben lived half a mile from the bridge that
Jonny lived under. Every day on his walk to
school, Ben passed over the bridge. He
would always jump out and say, "Who's that
walking on my bridge!" in a big gruff voice.
Ben would say, "It's just me, Ben."
Then Jonny would invite Ben to come under
the bridge to play for a little bit before he went
to school.

Jonny had a cool little place to live under the
bridge. He had a box for a table and a tree
stump for a chair. There was on old TV that
he had fixed up himself. He kept the wind and
rain off of himself by nailing a tarp under the

bridge and a piece of wood. Trolls don't get that cold anyway. Even though Jonny lived under a bridge and was very poor but Ben didn't care. He liked Jonny just how he was. So many people act like they're your friend but they're not.

Then when Ben came home from school every day they would play and play for hours. Jonny was the only friend Ben could ever want in the whole wide world. They were so happy talking and playing their favorite game kickball. The bases were big, flat rocks and Ben had brought an old ball from home. Ben always let Jonny win.

Ben's mom questioned Jonny about where he was spending all of his time. Ben told his mom about Jonny and that he had no friends and that he lived under a bridge. Ben's mom was concerned. She called the police and the police said it wasn't a *person* living under the bridge…it was a huge animal of some sort. The police were alarmed so they called animal control.

Ben tried to explain to everyone and his mom that Ben wasn't a human mortal but he was from long ago. Somehow he had survived and wound up living under the bridge. He was very nice and wouldn't hurt a fly.

Ben never saw him again. He guessed that animal control took him away. Ben convinced his mom to go with him to visit Jonny in at the dog pound. They talked to Jonny and even though he was in a cage, he looked happy to see Ben *and* his mom. His mom decided to help Jonny get out.

One day, the guard was sleeping against the bars of the cell. Ben and his mom were coming to visit and saw their chance to get Jonny out. Ben took the keys out of the guards pocket and put them in the lock and got Jonny out.

He went home with Ben and played for several hours. When the dog pound came looking for Jonny, they just said that Jonny was their new pet. The dog pound was happy because Jonny was eating too much at the pound and costing them a lot of money. Ben said, "I think we should be friends forever!"

"Yeah," said Jonny cheerfully. From that day forward everybody that met Jonny said they wanted to be his friend. And they lived happily ever after.

They took over the dog pound and rescued many hurt and abused animals. They became famous and the town even built a monument and proclaimed a day after them. Instead of having Tuesday…it is Benday.

Mount Everest Elementary Bully Drama
By: Tyler Wheatley

There once was a girl named Katie. She was very poor and she had blue eyes, and raggedy clothes and not very cute. But she was very nice to other people. Also she had no friends at school and she hated it. The teachers where very mean at Mt. Everest Elementary.

One day [last day of school] at MEES {Mount Everest Elementary School}, Katie was walking down the hallway. Jason was walking down behind HER [one of the bullies] and ran up on her and grabbed her. He pushed her against the wall saying, "You better tell the principal you look ugly! Katie you are stupid. If you don't I'll stick your head down the toilet!"

Katie said, "Please don't hurt me. This is the last day of school and its Field Day."

Jason said, "I don't care you are ugly."

But at the moment. The teacher said, "Are you ready to go run for Field Day?"

The kid's said, "We are absolutely ready!" But Katie just sat there. She did not want to race against the 2 mean kids, Jason and Taylor.

The teacher said, "Come on Katie. You are a good runner." Slowly Katie got up and got into the racing line.

Up for running were Katie, Jason, and Taylor. Jason +Taylor where the bullies. Katie was in the lead but she fell crying Jason passed her up saying, "you are stupid. "Taylor said, "Ha-ha you can't catch me." She was crying she laid there for 5 minutes the teacher didn't help at all she got up crying and told her mom her mom told her mom and her mom told the teacher the teacher told the principal and Taylor + Jason got suspended from school and couldn't go back and they all got split up and never saw each other any more.

I hope you liked my story.

THE END!!!!

E BOY

BY: Devin Williams

Hello this is Steve he has no home. He is in a virtual video game he is trying to build a house his only resource was wood so he built his house out of that. Now it is night creepers are coming. They blow up so Steve made a phone call. He called his brother his name is Herobrine. Steve said,(Pick me up!)
Now he at his brother's house. He thinks he's safe. When they wake up they build Steve a house.

Steve liked his house. But he had no bed so he looked for sheep to get wool. Steve turned around he saw a CREEPER! He ran to kill it but with what? He had no weapon's will he fight it?

Steve ran away to build a sword the creeper was following him. Later on he had built a sword. So he turned around to fight the creeper but there were 10 more. Then Steve climbed a tree so he called his brother to pick him up .Herobrine got there the creepers KILLED herobine. Steve cried

Steve walked along the next day he saw a big house. He saw someone farming it was his friend bill. Bill said "How goes there"
                    Steve said "Let's go kill those creepers".

Vacation Time
By: Hailey Zortman

Once there was a girl named Hailey and she
was 9 years old. She had brown hair and she
is really nice. Hailey lived on the beach.
She had so much fun and she loved playing
on the beach. She made sand castles and
played in the ocean.

She never wanted to go home when it when
her parents called her. She was also very
lazy and didn't want to clean the sand off of
her toys or herself.

It was time to go to home one day and her
mom said, "Clean all the sand off of
everything and we will go."

Hailey did not want to clean off things so
she didn't. Her mom saw that she was not
going to clean up and she reminded Hailey
of the choice she was making by not
following directions.

Hailey looked at her mom and all of the
sand she was going to have to clean up and
she packed all her stuff up without cleaning

the sand off. Her parents knew that Hailey would have to be taught a lesson. They let her get all the way to the car with her sandy toys. Her mom and dad took her and the toys and cleaned them all up. Then they said, " Hailey because of your bad choice you can't play with your I-pod or Kindle Fire or go to the beach for a week."

Hailey was very bored and sad for the rest of the week. Every time she would mention the beach, her parents would say, "This was your decision. You chose not to clean up your mess."

Hailey became very helpful around the house that week because she couldn't play with anything. She cleaned her room, helped her mom around the house. She even helped her dad out in the yard. Cleaning and being helpful turned out to be more fun than she expected. Plus her parents were not disappointed in her.

A week later, her mom asked Hailey if she wanted to go to the beach. Hailey said, "If we are finished with all of our jobs here at home then I think I would love to go to the beach."

Her parents gave back all of her electronic things and was glad that Hailey had learned that cleaning up after yourself is a good thing. Hailey was very happy.

THE END

Friends at the Beach
By: Sydney Cook

It was early one summers day at the beach. I was in line for the water slide. I looked behind me to see how far back the line was and then at that very moment I saw a boy that looked exactly like my best friend Jaden! But I didn't think it was him. I turned around and waited for my turn but I looked back at the boy for a second. And then I noticed that the boy was Jaden! And it only took a second for Jaden to notice that it was me. He looked down at me and asked, "Is your name Sydney?" and I said back, "Yes!" Who would have known that I saw my best friend at the beach!

The Gift
By: Ella Deweese

It was a nice winter day and I was prepared for Christmas and I really wanted a bow and arrow. On Christmas day I got gift. It was in red wrapping paper. It was a bow and arrow and I was so happy excited! "I got it! It's really here!" I went into the woods and I shot my bow and it was so fun cool! Now I use my bow all the time. I wasn't as good when I first started. Now I am so good! I am going to go deer hunting with my dad but I do not know if I will use my bow or not! I even got a hunting name. It is White Wind but I don't know if that's a real thing!

My Dog Died
By: Dalton Dockery

One day in early summer I was at my grandma and grandpas swimming in the pool. After fireworks in the day we went home. My sister Grace was playing with my dog.

My black lab attacked him. They fought. I looked in his eyes. He didn't move. He stood still. I cried my eyes out. He was the poorest dog in the world. I was the only one to take care of him. I was upset.

We buried him by a gate. Rocks and a wooden cross stood on top. My mom told me on the slide, "Don't worry. All of us will be like him."

We went home. We looked at pictures of Vinnie. I told God, "Will Vinnie come back?" Gold told me no. I was crying so loud and smooth like rain.

So he is looking down at me. My dog is probably happy where he is right now. I hope he has a very happy family up in heaven. I was very upset when Vinnie died. He was my best dog friend in the whole wide world. My dog must be sleeping right now. I hope he has a fun time.

I Went in the Water
By: Brennan Gray

I went in the water. I went on a small boat. I, me, and my mom. And we went fast. We were dranking juices. I almost fell off the their boat. There was no seatbelts. We went over a bridge. There was bats. We fished. We went in the water. There was a shark. It was very big. My mom got in the boat. I couldn't. I got attacked. I got to safety. My mom said, "Never do that again!" It was the Ohio Bridge.

My Dog Passed Away
By: Landon Hutsell

One early morning I went to my mom's and dad's room. Then I said, "Good morning." Then I went downstairs. Then I saw my dog laying down and suffering. She was brown and white. She had a tumor in her heart. My eyes were wet. My dog was pooing on the floor. It was stinky, smelly brown poo. Her name was Mema. Then I went back up stairs. Then I said, "My dog pooed on the floor." My mom went downstairs then cleaned it up. My dog couldn't get up. Then my mom's eyes were wet. Then my little brother said, "Eee, poo is in the floor." Then my dad came down stairs and gave her fresh air. My dad gave her water. My dog did not drank it. Then I started crying. Then my mom taked her to the hospital. They got her medicine. Then she passed away on my mom's hands. I cried, cried, cried, cried, cried, really, really hard. I miss my dog very much but she's in heaven a better place to live.

The Hug
By: Kylie Hilton

It was Valentine's Day and Daddy got me a bouquet of flowers. They were all different colors. They smelled good. It was a warm winters night and he gave me a hug on the check. And he cuddled with me. And everybody hugged me. I felt loving. He and Mommy snuggled with me in a blanket. I almost smiled. What will you do if your Daddy acts like that?

Football Days
By: Jaden Smith

It was a warm sunny summer day when my team was practicing and I was running the ball. Our jerseys were black and blue. And eight people were on my team and eight people were on another team. And we played until 8:00 pm and I got a touchdown and we won the tournament! Before we got the big trophy the sun was not out and the sky was darker than smoke. We went to the All Stars and we won that too! And I was happy when we won the tournament. And we got a big, big trophy and it came to Mt. Washington and we got two trophies for MWE because our team won. And we helped each other out and we had a mascot! And there is one All Star practice. And whoever wins the All Star game gets a big, big, big,, huge, huge, huge, tournament trophy!

The First Day of First Grade
By: Gracie Whitworth

It was one early beautiful summer day. It was the first day of school. The first thing we had to do was draw a picture. I drew me and my twin sister. My partners in my group drew beach balls. The teacher said to come to the rug. She said, "My name is Mrs. Miller." Then she said, "Now you get to see me, oh beautiful me!" I said in my head, "What would we do next?" She told us to take out our morning journals and write how we feel about the class. And after that we looked around. Then we sat on the carpet and talked about stuffed animals that we read with. Then I thought in my head, "Would it be like kindergarten?" But it was not. It was better! Mrs. Miller had fantastic activities throughout the whole day. She had games. It was fun, really, really, fun! By the end of the day, I felt good about my new teacher Mrs. Miller but I met a great buddy. Her name was Kylie. But the good

news was my best friend from
kindergarten will always be my best friend.

When My Pa Died
By: Taylor Young

Young Authors District Winner 2013

It was one late night. The stars were shining. It was long past my bedtime. I was going to my Nanny's and when we got there I ran into her house to see her and in her living room I saw a hospital bed and nurse. My Pa was in the bed.

I felt sad because I have heard that he had very, very, very bad cancer. And I was about to cry when I started to touch his hand. It was hard to swallow. I felt so sad I had to leave the room.

Well, a couple of days later I went back to my Nanny's and Pa was still in the bed because of the cancer. My mom had told me that he died. I felt very nervous.

I miss my Pa very much but he is still in heaven, a better place for him to live. But he is still alive in heaven. My mental image of heaven is angels everywhere and fluffy clouds. I still have him right by my side every day. My mom said, "Everything is going to be alright." And it was.